DISCOVERING ISLAM with MUSTAFA

S. J. SEAR

AuthorHouse™ UK
1663 Liberty Drive
Bloomington, IN 47403 USA
www.authorhouse.co.uk
UK TFN: 0800 0148641 (Toll Free inside the UK)
UK Local: 02036 956322 (+44 20 3695 6322 from outside the UK)

Because of the dynamic nature of the Internet, any web addresses or links contained in this book may have changed
since publication and may no longer be valid. The views expressed in this work are solely those of the author and do
not necessarily reflect the views of the publisher, and the publisher hereby disclaims any responsibility for them.

Any people depicted in stock imagery provided by Getty Images are models,
and such images are being used for illustrative purposes only.
Certain stock imagery © Getty Images.

This book is printed on acid-free paper.

ISBN: 978-1-6655-9322-9 (sc)
ISBN: 978-1-6655-9321-2 (e)

Print information available on the last page.

Published by AuthorHouse 10/08/2021

authorHOUSE®

Contents

Names of Allah

ar-Rahman
The Lord of Mercy

ar-Raheem
The Giver of Mercy

al-Malik
The Absolute Ruler

al-Quddus
The Pure One

as-Salaam
The Source of Peace

al-Mu'min
The Guardian of Faith

al-Muhaymin
The Protector

al-Azeez
The Mighty

al-Jabbar
The Compeller

al-Mutakabbir
The Majestic

al-Khaliq
The Creator

al-Bari
The Evolver

al-Musawwir
The Fashioner

al-Ghaffar
The Forgiver

al-Qahhar
The One Who Subdues

al-Wahhab
The Great Giver

ar-Razzak
The Provider

al-Fattah
The Granter of Success

al-Aleem
The All-Knowing

al-Qabid
The One Who Restrains

al-Basit
The Expander

al-Khafid
The Abaser

ar-Rafi
The Exalter

al-Mu'izz
The Honourer

al-Muzill
The Dishonourer

as-Sami
The All-Hearing

al-Baseer
The All-Seeing

al-Hakam
The Judge

al-'Adil
The Just

al-Latif
The Most Subtle

al-Khabir The All-Aware	**al-Kareem** The Most Generous	**al-Qawi** The Most Strong
al-Haleem The Forbearing One	**al-Raqeeb** The Watchful One	**al-Mateen** The Firm One
al-Azeem The Great One	**al-Mujeeb** The Responder	**al-Waali** The Governor
al-Ghafur The All-Forgiving	**al-Wasi'** The All-Embracing	**al-Hameed** The Praiseworthy
ash-Shakur The Most Appreciative	**al-Hakeem** The Most Wise	**al-Muhsi** The Reckoner
al-'Ali The Most High	**al-Wadud** The Loving	**al-Mubdi** The Originator
al-Kabir The Most Great	**al-Majid** The Most Glorious	**al-Mu'id** The Restorer
al-Hafiz The Preserver	**al-Ba'ith** The Resurrector	**al-Muhyi** The Giver of Life
al-Muqeet The Maintainer	**ash-Shahid** The Witness	**al-Mumit** The Creator of Death
al-Haseeb The Reckoner	**al-Haq** The Truth	**al-Hayy** The Ever Living One
al-Jalil The Sublime One	**al-Wakil** The Trustee	**al-Qayyum** The Self-Existing One

al-Wajid **The Finder**	**al-Bateen** **The Hidden**	**al-Ghani** **The Self-Sufficient**
al-Majid **The Noble**	**al-Wali** **The Protecting Friend**	**al-Mughni** **The Enricher**
al-Wahid **The Unique**	**al-Muta'ali** **The Most Exalted**	**al-Mani** **The Preventer**
al-Ahad **The One**	**al-Barr** **The Source of All Good**	**ad-Darr** **The Afflicter**
as-Samad **The Eternal**	**al-Tawwab** **Acceptor of Repentance**	**an-Nafi** **The Source of Good**
al-Qadir **The Able One**	**al-Muntaqim** **The Avenger**	**an-Nur** **The Light**
al-Muqtadir **The Creator of Power**	**al-Afuw** **The Pardoner**	**al-Hadi** **The Guide**
al-Muqaddim **The Expediter**	**ar-Ra'uf** **The Compassionate**	**al-Badi** **The Incomparable**
al-Mu'akhkhir **The Delayer**	**Malik-ul-Mulk** **Eternal Sovereign Lord**	**al-Baqi** **The Everlasting**
al-Awwal **The First**	**Dul-Jalal-Wal-Ikram** **Lord of Majesty, Bounty**	**al-Warith** **The Supreme Inheritor**
al-Akhir **The Last**	**al-Muqseet** **The Most Equitable**	**ar-Rashid** **Guide to the Right Path**
az-Zaheer **The Manifest**	**al-Jami'** **The Gatherer**	**as-Sabur** **The Patient, Steadfast**

If you learn the Arabic names of **Allah** you can then call Him by them when you pray. Learn the meanings, too, but keep in mind that translations often do not and sometimes cannot convey the exact Arabic meaning and that many names have multiple meanings. For example, as-Samad means, *The Eternal*, but it also means, *The One Who Satisfies Every Need, The One All Depend Upon, The One Who Is Unaffected, Unchanged and Without Any Needs*, and more besides.

Early Days

As-salaamu-alaikum! My name is Mustafa, and I am about to embark on a wonderful journey to learn and discover as much as I can. In other words, I shall soon be off to school. So, come along and learn with me. It will be very interesting and well worthwhile, I promise you. It will be fun, too.

Like everyone's journey, mine began the day I was born. My mum said I was the most beautiful baby in the world, but I guess all mums say that.

It was raining. It was also **Jummah** (Friday), a special day of the week for Muslims, a **Muslim** being someone who follows the religion of **Islam**. The word Islam means peace and submission to God.

Grandad, the head of our family, was one of the first to greet me. His long beard must have brushed against my tiny face as he held me close to recite **adhan** and then **iqamah**. Adhan is the Muslim call to prayer. Iqamah is the announcement that prayers in the mosque are about to begin.

He recited adhan in my right ear and iqamah in my left ear, which is the Muslim way of welcoming a new-born baby into the world and into the fold of Islam. Grandad said the words ever so softly because I was so very small.

A few days later, I was given the name Mustafa, which means *Chosen One*. Mustafa is also one of the many names of **Prophet Muhammad**, **sallallahu alayhi wasallam** (peace and praise of Allah be upon him). Remember to say this blessing whenever you mention his name.

In Arabic, the blessing is written like this: ﷺ

Mum said I was a very happy baby and loved it when she sang her special lullaby. It had only one word, **Allah**, which she sang over and over until I fell asleep. She wanted Allah to be the first word I would say. And it was! Amidst babbling and gurgling, and to everyone's surprise, I actually said it several times. Dad told me Mum was so happy, she cried.

Allah is the greatest name of God and the one we use most often. God has countless names that describe His attributes, but we only know those mentioned in the **Holy Quran** or told by Prophet Muhammad ﷺ to whom the Quran and the religion of Islam were revealed.

As I am sure you have already guessed, my learning began in the cradle. Whether I was asleep or wide awake, cooing and gurgling as babies do, my mum would quietly recite verses from the Holy Quran and would often sing:

🎵 "La ilaha illallah; Muhammadur-rasulullah." 🎵

(None has the right to be worshipped but Allah; Muhammad is the Prophet of Allah). Known as **Kalimah Tayyab** (Word of Purity), it is the first of the six **kalimah** of Islam, the fundamentals of a Muslim's beliefs.

Does your mum ever say, "Behave yourself!" or "Be good!"? My mum does. She says it all the time. And I remember once, when I was very small, she sat me on her lap and said, "Always be careful what you say and do, Mustafa!"

She then placed her finger on my lips and sang:

♫ "Be careful little lips what you say!" ♫

I looked up at her, wide-eyed with wonder. "Think before you speak, Mustafa, and try to say good things," she explained. "Always speak the truth and never say rude, unkind or hurtful things."

Next, she held my hands and sang:

♫ "Be careful little hands what you do!" ♫

"Use your hands to work and play and make wonderful things. Never use them to steal or hurt anyone."

She then tickled my toes and sang:

♫ "Be careful little feet where you tread!" ♫

"Use your feet to walk and run and play. Never use them to hurt anyone or harm any living thing."

She told me a story about a little boy who thought it was fun to tread on bugs and other creepy things. His name was Toppit. Not his real name of course but a pet name given to him because when he was learning to talk, instead of "Stop it!" he would say "Top it!"

Well, one day, Toppit found some snails in the garden, and you can guess what he did next, can't you. He trod on them and crushed them, every single one. That night, however, he had a very disturbing dream. He dreamt he was playing in the garden when a huge bumblebee suddenly appeared. It flew directly towards him and settled on the ground just inches away, but as he raised his foot to stamp on it, it mysteriously disappeared.

Toppit looked around, wondering where it had gone. Suddenly, it reappeared and began to circle above his head, buzzing so noisily Toppit thought his eardrums

would burst. He put his hands over his ears to shut out the deafening sound, and closed his eyes, wishing the pesky creature would go away.

After a while, he dared to open his eyes only to discover the bumblebee was hovering in front of him, completely silent now, but so close he could see its eyes. They were big and bright, and full of tears.

"The snails were my friends. They never did you any harm, so why did you kill them? Why? Why? Why?"

The bumblebee's mournful cries of "Why? Why? Why?" echoed around the garden as it flew off, leaving a long trail of sparkling tear-drops behind.

Toppit then realised that even the tiniest of creatures have intelligence; and that like us, they also feel pain.

"I'm sorry!" he called out. "I'm really sorry I hurt your friends. I will never, ever harm any creature again. I promise!"

At once, the woeful echoing stopped, and the sparkling trail of tears turned into the most beautiful rainbow Toppit had ever seen.

Happy Schooldays

Hurray! I'm finally off to school. An Islamic school! So, as well as learning arithmetic, science, and other subjects, I shall also be learning about Islam. I have an amazing teacher and I think she likes me because she said I am one of the brightest boys in her class. I told her I am always keen to learn and say **Bismillah** before I begin my work.

Bismillah means, (I begin) with the Name of God, and is the first part of the phrase, **Bismillah ir-Rahman ir-Rahim**, (I begin) with the name of God, the Lord of Mercy, the Giver of Mercy.

My grandma once told me a story to help me remember to say Bismillah. It may help you, too. It is about a mother bird and her fledglings.

Three little birds, Bobby, Ben, and Henry were having their very first flying lesson. "Now, it's really quite simple," their mother explained. "First say Bismillah, flap your wings, and then leap into the air."

Little Henry pushed forward. "Like this!" he chirped, leaping from the nest.

Everyone watched in horror as he plummeted towards the ground. Foolish, daredevil Henry! Not only did he forget to say Bismillah, but he also forgot to flap his wings. Lucky for him, he landed on a heap of dead leaves, dazed and bewildered but otherwise unhurt.

It was Bobby's turn next. He was so excited, he also forgot to say Bismillah. And he made the big mistake of looking down at the ground below, which made him so dizzy he spun around and forgot which way he was facing. Undeterred, he spread his wings and dived, only to land in his own nest.

While his mother was busy scolding him, Ben clambered to the edge of the nest. He was the youngest but by far the brightest, full of ambition, and eager to fly the nest and explore the world.

Remembering his mother's words, he boldly chirped, "Bismillah," and spread his tiny wings. He then leapt from the nest, flapped his tiny wings, and took to the air as if he had been flying all his life.

After flitting joyfully from tree to tree, he returned to the nest to help his brothers so they too could enjoy the world.

I say Bismillah before I begin any work or eat or drink anything; and afterwards I say **Alhamdulillah** (all praise belongs to God). It is my way of thanking Allah, for I know He alone gives me health and strength to work and play. He alone provides me with everything I need.

Giving charity is also a way of thanking Allah. Every year, there is a charity day at school, and in our local mosque we have two charity boxes, a small one for money and a big one for clothes and other useful things.

The other day, Mum and Dad decided to sort out the loft to see if there was anything worth giving away. And wow! It was crammed with books and toys and bric-a-brac. Things we no longer needed!

Dad was really excited. "Do you know what!" he said. "If we get rid of all this stuff, we could convert the loft into a nice study room for you, Mustafa. What do you think?"

I thought it was a great idea, so did Mum, so we gave everything away, except for a very pretty pot with a lid. It was just what I needed for collecting my pocket money in.

⁂

Now, guess what happened on the way to school? I found a bird lying on the footpath. At first, I thought it was dead, but then it blinked its tiny eyes, so I carefully picked it up and held it gently against my chest. The poor thing was trembling with cold, and I wanted so much to take care of it, but it was school time, so I had to give it to my dad to take home.

Now, I think I might be allergic to birds or feathers or something because in class my nose began to itch. I rubbed then wiggled and twitched it, hoping no one would see me and think I was making rude faces at them. And then I sneezed. Not once, not twice, but *seven* times. So loudly, my best friend Humza who sits next to me almost fell off his seat, and Amina, who's as timid as a mouse, screamed her head off.

Even worse, Teacher stared at me as if I had set off a box of fireworks or thrown a bomb or something.

And then everyone in class got the giggles. And I mean everyone!

Teacher's great, though. She didn't tell us off. And when all was quiet, she told us some very interesting facts about sneezing.

"Sneezing is actually a good thing because it expels dust and germs trapped inside the nostrils and, as you know, germs can make us ill," she explained.

"But remember, *coughs and sneezes spread diseases*, especially in crowded places like a classroom. So, whenever you sneeze, cover your nose and mouth with a tissue or handkerchief if you have one, or use the crook of your elbow, and then say Alhamdulillah! Those who hear you should say, **Yarhamuk Allah**! (May Allah have mercy on you!)."

Teacher also told us to say **Insha'Allah** (if Allah wills it) whenever we wish for anything or intend to do something. She says not even a leaf falls from a tree unless Allah wills it.

When I got home, I asked Mum and Dad if the little bird would get better and they both replied, "Insha'Allah!"

We kept it in a cardboard box with a few holes in the sides for air. We put some straw on the bottom to keep it warm, a little pot of clean drinking water, and a dish of breadcrumbs mixed with bird seed. It quickly recovered, so we set it free, hoping it would find its family and friends.

I have many friends, and instead of saying *hello*, which doesn't really mean anything, I greet them with **As-salaamu-alaikum**! (Peace be with you!), and my friends then say **Wa-alaikum as-salaam**! (And Peace be with you, too!).

Some Muslims, like my grandad, extend the greeting to **As-salaamu alaikum wa-rahmatullahi wa-barakatuh!** (Peace and mercy of Allah and His blessings be with you!) and reply with **Wa-alaikum as-salaam wa-rahmatullahi wa-barakatuh!** (Peace and mercy of Allah and His blessings be with you, too!).

Many people from other parts of the world live in our neighbourhood. I have two African friends, Kofi, and Omari. They live close by, and we often play together in the park. They are both great fun to be with, forever smiling; and I love their dark skin, sparkly white teeth, and frizzy hair. Kofi shakes my hand, but Omari always greets me with a friendly bear hug. Some people don't welcome newcomers. But my dad says we are all Allah's creation and children of Adam, whatever our colour or creed. That is why Islam teaches us to be kind to everyone and respectful of their religion, customs, and beliefs.

Forever Learning

Great news! I have been promoted to the next class. The work is more difficult, but I have learnt a little prayer to help me: **Ya rubbi zidnee ilmaa**! (O' Lord, increase my knowledge!). After saying Bismillah, I recite this prayer.

In the Quran, it says that if all the trees on earth were pens, and all the water in the sea with seven seas added was ink, it still would not be enough to write Allah's knowledge. Limitless knowledge! So it seems I shall be forever learning. But I don't mind. I enjoy learning. I learn something new every day.

Allah also tells us to travel to all the corners of the world in search of knowledge. I walk to school every day and that's quite a long way for me, but Insha'Allah when I'm older, I shall travel far and see wonderful places, like the mountain resort Dad took us to last summer.

Our cabin overlooked a beautiful lake that sparkled in the sun like a huge bowl of emeralds fringed with tall, majestic pine trees. And in the distance, there was a snow-capped mountain, its craggy peaks appearing and disappearing, playing hide-and-seek with the clouds.

We would sit on the veranda, admiring the scenic splendour, and have endless fun finding figures and faces in the silently drifting clouds.

"Dad! This place is awesome," I exclaimed.

"**Subhan'Allah**!" he replied. "When we see something wonderful, we should always say *Subhan'Allah* (Glorified is Allah), or **Masha'Allah** (Whatever Allah wills or decides)."

Allah created the entire universe, as well as all the creatures, great and small. He alone is the Creator and makes everything as it pleases Him. So, if we love Him we must also love His Creation, which means the people we live with, all the animals around us, and even tiny creatures like spiders.

I used to be terrified of spiders, but now I actually like them because Allah saved Prophet Muhammad's life with the help of tiny spider. Here is the story.

Muhammad ﷺ once had to hide in a cave to escape his own clansmen, the Quraysh, who had become his worst enemies because he preached Islam, urging them to leave their idols and worship Allah alone.

They believed in Allah, that He was their Creator and Provider, but they also believed they could only reach Him through their idols. To abandon them was thus unthinkable, so they decided to kill Muhammad ﷺ and silence him once and for all. But where was he?

They searched the highways and the byways but could find no sign of him. Suspecting he might have taken refuge in the Cave of Thaur, the Quraysh scouts climbed up the steep slopes and were about to search inside.

Just inches away from their feet, Muhammad ﷺ and his faithful friend, Abu Bakr, were crouching, silent and still, hardly daring to breathe. Miraculously however, the entrance had been covered over by a spider's web.

"He can't possibly be in there," said one of the scouts. "This cobweb looks as if it has been here for ages, long before Muhammad was born."

So, convinced that no one could possibly be hiding in the cave, the scouts hurriedly made their way back down the slopes to search elsewhere.

Today was a great day for me. Teacher asked me to name the principles of Islam, known as the Five Pillars of Islam, and I knew them all by heart.

1. **Shahada**: declaration of faith, the belief in the Oneness of God.
2. **Salah**: the five daily prayers all Muslims must perform.
3. **Zakat**: money Muslims must give for the poor and needy.
4. **Saum**: fasting from sunrise to sunset for the entire month of Ramadhan.
5. **Hajj**: the pilgrimage to Mecca in the month of Dhul Hijjah.

Teacher was so pleased; she gave me my first golden star. Mum's always reminding me to be polite so, with a smile that must have filled my face, I said, "Thank you, Teacher."

"**Jazakallahu khairan**, Mustafa," she said. "If we say *Jazakallahu khairan* (May Allah reward you with goodness) our thanks become a blessing, too."

Do you know there are about forty different calendars in use in the world today? Most countries use the Gregorian calendar, which has 365 days in a year and is based on the movements of the sun. The Islamic calendar has only 354 or 355 days and is based on the movements of the moon.

Months of the Islamic Calendar

1.	**Muharram**	7.	**Rajab**
2.	**Safar**	8.	**Shaban**
3.	**Rabi ul Awwal**	9.	**Ramadhan**
4.	**Rabi ul Thani**	10.	**Shawwal**
5.	**Jamada al Ula**	11.	**Dhul Qadah**
6.	**Jamada al Thania**	12.	**Dhul Hijjah**

We had to memorise them, so I said my special prayer, Ya rubbi zidnee ilmaa! (O' Lord, increase my knowledge!), and managed to learn them all.

"I wish I had a brain like yours," said Humza. "Mine's worse than a sieve."

I laughed, thinking he was joking as he so often does, but Humza's face was very serious, which worried me.

"Cheer up! Your brain is fine," I assured him. "It's probably just a little rusty. Mine is too, sometimes. No one's perfect."

I told him about my special prayer, and then a story about an old woman who used to fetch water for her family from the village well.

Every day, she would fill two large earthen pots, but one of them had a crack in it, slowly trickling water, so by the time she reached home it was only half full.

One day, a neighbour noticed the crack. "That pot is useless. It's always half empty," he moaned. "You should throw it away and get a new one."

But the old woman disagreed.

"It's not useless. You may think it's half empty, but I know it's always half full, and despite the crack it's a very useful pot. Come! Let me show you."

She then led him to the well, and all along the way there were beautiful flowers in bloom. "Both pots hold enough water for our daily use," she said, "but the cracked one gives water to the flowers, too. So you see, it's really very useful. Everything is useful. Everything and everyone have a purpose."

Humza smiled and said I'm the best friend ever. I like it when he smiles. It means he's happy, and that makes me happy, too.

Do you know the names and times of the daily prayers?

The first is called **Fajr** – early in the morning before the sun rises.
The second is called **Zuhr** – midday when the sun is high in the sky.
The third is called **Asr** – middle of the afternoon.

The fourth is called **Maghrib** – after sunset when the sun has gone down.

The fifth and last daily prayer is called **Isha** – at night-time, before going to sleep.
Some Muslims get up in the middle of the night to say a special prayer called

Tahajjud. All five daily prayers are compulsory, but if we miss the Fajr or Asr prayers we risk losing the blessings we have earned. So beware!

There was once a very powerful king and prophet who almost lost his kingdom because he missed the Asr prayer. His name was **Sulaiman** (Solomon, **alayhi salaam**, Peace be upon him!). Exceptionally intelligent and wise, Sulaiman was often wiser than his illustrious father, **King Dawud** (David, alayhi salaam), also a prophet. An illustration of his wisdom is when a shepherd and a farmer came to the royal court with a dispute.

During the night, the shepherd's goats had wandered into the farmer's field and ruined all the crops, so the farmer demanded compensation. Since the value of the goats was about equal to the value of the crops they had destroyed, King Dawud ordered the shepherd to give all his goats to the farmer, which according to the law was a just decision.

However, as they were leaving the palace they met Sulaiman who asked them if their dispute had been settled. When they told him about the king's decision, Sulaiman remarked, "If I had judged this case, my verdict would have been different and would have benefitted both of you."

He then went to his father. "Wouldn't it be more reasonable if the herd of goats were given to the farmer so he could benefit from their milk and offspring, and the field given to the shepherd so he could cultivate and grow crops?" he explained. "And when the field is as it was before the goats strayed into it, then the property of both men should be returned to them."

King Dawud heartily agreed and called the men back to court. He then gave a new judgment according to his son's ingenious suggestion.

Besides great wisdom, Allah endowed Sulaiman with the power to control the winds. The jinn also obeyed him. And as well as soldiers, he had many animals and birds in his massive army. A mighty king for sure! But he had one great weakness that almost cost him his throne. A passion for horses!

One afternoon, he was so engrossed, stroking and admiring his horses, he missed the Asr prayer. So, to reprimand him, Allah took his throne away. Overcome with shame and sorrow, Sulaiman prayed, earnestly begging forgiveness. Sometime later, Allah restored him to the throne and blessed him with a dominion like no other.

The Best Things in Life

When I was born, my grandad greeted me with **adhan** and **iqamah**. Of course I don't remember. And who knows how much babies can understand? I often hear adhan and wanted to know what Allah says when He calls us to prayer, so here are the Arabic words and their meanings.

<u>Adhan</u>

Allahu Akbar! Allah is the Greatest! (recite four times)

Ash hadu al-la ilaha ill'Allah! I bear witness that there is no deity but Allah! (recite twice)

Ash-hadu anna Muhammad ur-rasul Allah! I bear witness that Muhammad is the Prophet of Allah! (recite twice)

Hayya 'alas salah! Come to prayer! (recite twice)

Hayya 'alal falah! Come to success! (recite twice)

Allahu Akbar! Allah is the Greatest! (recite twice)

La ilaha ill'Allah! There is no deity but Allah! (recite once)

<u>Iqamah</u>

Qad qamatis salah! The prayer has begun! (recite twice)

Adhan is given five times a day, before each of the five daily prayers. Adhan for Fajr prayer, however, is slightly different. After the words, *Hayya 'alal falah*, the following sentence is added and recited twice: **Assalatu khayrum minan naum** (prayer is better than sleep).

When someone comes to wake me up, I usually dive under the covers, but I know I shouldn't. If we leave the comfort of our bed or any other pleasure to say our prayers at the proper time, we can be hopeful of His forgiveness and blessings. If we are lazy or careless, we gain nothing.

Some people say the best things in life are free, and others say the best things are money and fame. My dad believes the best things in life are complete faith in Allah and striving to earn His pleasure; and the absolute worst is to earn His displeasure. That's why I try my best to be good.

My dad is good and kind. He is very brave, too. Where we live, he is the local hero. Last winter, there was a violent storm, and several trees were uprooted by the gale-force winds. An old tree in a neighbour's back garden was one of them. Dad was looking out from an upstairs window at the time and saw it come crashing down onto their kitchen roof.

Despite the howling wind and blinding rain, he grabbed his raincoat and rushed over to see if they needed any help. I wanted to go with him, but he wouldn't let me. He said it was too dangerous.

Luckily, everyone was okay, but the children were very upset. "Uncle, please can you get Toffee," they pleaded.

"Toffee is their pet rabbit," their mum explained. "She's just a baby, and we're worried because her cage has been blown over."

Dad lost no time. Out he went, and after struggling to get a firm hold on the rain-drenched cage, he managed to get it upright. Toffee was huddled in the corner of the nest box, trembling with cold and fear, but otherwise unharmed. The children were delighted, as you can well imagine.

A few days later, their dad, who had been away at the time, came to our house to thank us. He gave us a cake his wife had baked especially for us. Chocolate cake with cream and strawberries on top! My absolute favourite!

A New Teacher

Do you like going to school? I do! In fact, I love school. But the other day, I didn't want to go. I was very upset because my favourite teacher was leaving. Dad said I had to go, and Mum said I should not get upset about changes or new things. She says life is full of changes and we should learn to accept them.

Anyway, I'm glad I did go because guess what? Our new teacher is a man. And he's simply awesome! I like him a lot. The whole class does. He has a big, friendly smile and is like an encyclopaedia, absolutely loaded with information. We've secretly named him Mr Google, but of course in class we all call him *Sir*.

Do you remember the Five Pillars of Islam – **Shahada**, **Salah**, **Zakat**, **Saum** and **Hajj**? Well, Sir has been telling us about each one in more detail.

SHAHADA – the first Pillar of Islam

It is the belief that there is only One God, Allah, Lord of the entire universe, and that none has the right to be worshipped but He. Kalimah Tayyab is a declaration of this belief and that Muhammad ﷺ is His Prophet (Rasul).

SALAH – the second Pillar of Islam

Salah means prayer. Prayer is a very important part of our lives. That is why it is one of the principles of Islam. Remember the five daily prayers?

Fajr, the prayer before sunrise; Zuhr, the midday prayer; Asr, the afternoon prayer; Maghrib, the prayer just after sunset; and Isha, the night-time prayer.

A **muezzin** is the person who gives adhan, the call to prayer. He stands facing **qiblah**, raises his hands to his ears and recites adhan in a loud voice. Adhan used to be given from a mosque's minaret, but nowadays a loudspeaker usually ensures everyone can hear. Qiblah is the direction towards the **Kaaba** in Mecca that all Muslims face when they pray.

Every Friday, there is a special congregational prayer in the mosque called **Jummah** prayer. Prayers commence with **khutbah**, a sermon delivered by the **imam**, the leader of the mosque.

Although prayer times are fixed, based on the position of the sun, the actual clock time for each prayer varies from day to day. That is because the times of sunrise and sunset gradually change throughout the year, according to the seasons and where we live in the world.

In class, we have been learning about **taharah**, spiritual purity. Before a Muslim prays, he must perform a special ablution known as **wudu**.

"Wudu is not a meaningless ritual," Sir explained. "It helps to purify us, not only physically but spiritually, so that we may come closer to Allah when we pray. It is also important to be dressed in decent, clean clothes. Men must cover at least part of their body from the navel to the knees, but women must cover their entire body except face and hands. Routine performance of wudu helps to ward off the devil, as well as common ailments like coughs and colds."

"Children should be taught and encouraged to pray at the age of seven," Sir continued, "but when they reach adolescence, prayer is compulsory."

Sir then demonstrated each step of wudu, without any water of course, the way Prophet Muhammad ﷺ taught his followers.

For some unknown reason, Humza and I had the giggles that day and began to fool around. I turned on an imaginary tap and pretended to do wudu, splashing water on Humza, making him dodge. And that was our game. I splashed, and he dodged. But then Humza lost his balance, toppled his chair, and ended up on the floor, legs in the air, which everyone found hilarious. And that is when, to our horror, we realized Sir had been watching us all the time.

Humza and I felt awful. Like it was the worst day of our lives! We apologized straight away, but Sir didn't say a word, nor did he smile.

HOW TO DO WUDU

* Wash your hands. First say *Bismillah* aloud or silently, then use the left hand to wash the right hand (do 3 times). Then use the right hand to wash the left hand (do 3 times). Be sure to wash in between the fingers and up to the wrists.

*Rinse your mouth. Use the right hand to cup water into your mouth, swish it around and to the back of throat, then spit it out (do 3 times).

*Clean your nose. Use your right hand to cup water into your nose, and then blow it out (do 3 times).

*Wash your face. Wash your face, spreading your hands from the right ear to the left and from the forehead to the chin (do 3 times).

*Wash your lower arms. Use the left hand to wash the right arm, wrist to elbow (3 times); then use the right hand to wash the left arm (3 times).

*Clean your head. With wet hands, wipe your forehead from eyebrows upwards, then over your hair, back of neck and temples (do once).

*Clean your ears. With wet hands, wipe both ears inside and out, using fingers to clean all crevices. Use the thumbs to clean behind the ears from the bottom upwards (do once).

*Wash your feet. Wash each foot (3 times, right foot first) up to the ankles, and between the toes, using the small finger to remove any dirt. Finally, point the right index finger skywards and recite a prayer of witness. The prayer is generally **Kalimah Shahadat**:

Ashahado an laa ilaha ill'Allaho; wahdahoo laa shareeka lahoo, wa-ashado anna Muhammadan abdo hoo wa rasullohoo. *I bear witness that there is no deity but Allah; He is One; He has no partner; and I bear witness that Muhammad is His servant and prophet.*

Forgive and Forget

A new day and a new lesson! And it seems Sir has completely forgotten about our tomfoolery the day before. But Sir is like that, always kind and forgiving.

He once told us that not to forgive and forget is like collecting heavy stones in your heart. They weigh you down. Forgiveness is one of Allah's qualities. He is **al-Ghafur** (the All-Forgiving). We are not true Muslims if we cannot forgive others, as well as ourselves.

"Today's lesson is about salah," he began in his usual, friendly way. "Of course, we can pray and talk to Allah anywhere, anytime, and in any language, but salah is a disciplined form of prayer and an essential part of worship."

In mosques worldwide, most Muslims recite salah in Arabic. For many, however, Arabic is not their mother tongue, so they memorise the words by heart. It is important to learn the meanings in our own language as well, so that we know exactly what we are saying when we pray.

HOW TO OFFER SALAH

1) <u>**Stand facing Qiblah, say which salah you intend to offer and then raise your hands to your ears saying:**</u> **Allahu Akbar** (Allah is the Greatest).

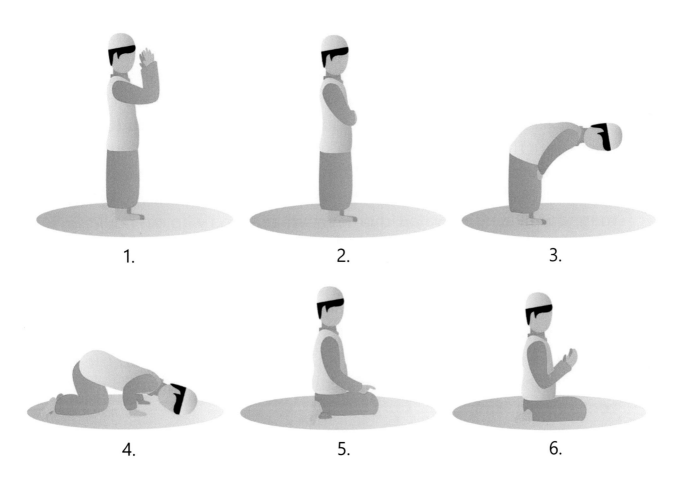

1. 2. 3.

4. 5. 6.

2) **Hold hands in front of your body, above or on the navel, with your right hand resting over your left hand, and recite:** **Subhana kalla humma waabi hamdaika** (O' Allah, Glorified, Praiseworthy), **watabara kas-muka wataala jadduka** (and blessed is Thy Name and exalted Thy Majesty), **wa la-ilaha ghairuk** (and there is no deity worthy of worship except Thee). **A'udhu billa hi minash shaitanir rajeem** (I seek refuge in Allah from the outcast Satan).

Recite Al-Fatihah, the opening Surah of the Quran: Bismillah ir-Rahman ir-Rahim (in the Name of Allah, the Extremely Merciful, the Lord of Mercy). **Alhamdulillahi rabbil-alamin ir-Rahman ir-Rahim**, (Praise be to Allah, Lord of all the Worlds, the Extremely Merciful, the Lord of Mercy), **malaiki yau mideen** (Master of the Day of Judgement). **Iyyaka n'abudu wa-iyyka nastaeen** (Thee alone we worship and to Thee alone we turn for help). **Ihdi nasiratal mustaqeem** (Guide us on the straight path), **siraataladhina an-amta alaihim** (the path of those whom You have favoured) **ghairil maghdoobi alaihim walad-dua-leen**, **ameen** (and who did not incur Your anger or go astray, O' Allah accept our prayer).

Recite Surah Al-Ikhlas or any other Surah: Bismillah ir-Rahman ir-Rahim (In the Name of Allah, the Extremely Merciful, the Lord of Mercy). **Qulhu wallahu ahad** (Say: He is the One and the only God). **Allah us-samad** (Allah the eternal upon whom all depend). **Lam yalid wa lam yulad** (He begets not, nor is He begotten). **Wa lam yakul lahu kufu-wan ahad** (None can be compared to Him).

3) **Bowing down to touch the knees say: Allahu Akbar** (Allah is the Greatest). **Subhana rabbi yal azim** (Glory to my Lord, the Great). Recite 3 times.

Then, coming back to standing position say: Sami Allahu'liman hamidah (Allah has heard all who praise Him). **Rabana lakal hamd** (Our Lord, praise be to Thee).

Allahu Akbar (Allah is the Greatest).

4) **Prostrate, forehead, knees, nose, and palms of hands touching the ground and say 3 times:** Subhana rabbi yal-a-ala (Glory to my Lord, the Highest).

5) **Say:** Allahu Akbar, **and then sit upright with knees still on the ground. After a pause say:** Allahu Akbar **and then prostrate as before and say 3 times:** Subhana rabbi yal-a-ala (Glory to my Lord, the Highest).

This completes one RAKAT. From standing to the two prostrations is one rakat.

The second rakat is the same except that when you sit upright you silently recite:

Aattahiyatu lil-lahi wa-salawaatu wat-tayibatu (All prayers and worship through words, actions and holiness are for Allah alone). **Asalaamu-alaika ayyuhan-nabiyyu** (Peace be with you, O Prophet), **wa rahmatul-lahi wa barakatuh** (and mercy of Allah and His blessings). **As-salaamu-alaina wa-ala ibadil lahisaliheen** (Peace be upon us and those who are righteous servants of Allah).

Ash-hadu al-la ilaha il'Allahu (I bear witness that there is no deity but Allah). **Wah wa-ashadu anna Muhammadan abduhu wa rasul Allah** (and I bear witness that Muhammad is His servant and Prophet). **Allah humma salli ala Muhammadin wa ala ali Muhammadin** (O' Allah, exalt Muhammad and the followers of Muhammad) **kama salaita ala Ibrahima wa ala ali Ibrahima** (as Thou did exalt Ibrahim and his followers). **Innaka hamidum majeed** (Thou art the Praised, the Glorious).

Allahuma barik ala Muhammadin (O' Allah, bless Muhammad) **wa ala ali Muhammadin** (and his followers) **kama barakta ala Ibrahima wa-ala ali**

Ibrahim (as Thou blessed Ibrahim and his followers). **Innaka Hamidum, Majeed** (Thou art the Praised, the Glorious).

Rabbij alni muqeimasalati wa min dhurriyyati (O' Lord! Make me and my offspring steadfast in prayer). **Rabbana wataqabal dua. Rabbanagh firli** (Our Lord! Accept my prayer. Our Lord! Forgive me), **wa liwalidayya wa lil-muminina yaumma yaqum-ul hisab** (and my parents and the believers on the Day of Judgement).

6) <u>**Turn your face to the right, saying:**</u> **Asalaamu-alaikum wa rahmat Allah** (Peace be with you and Allah's blessings).

<u>**And then turn your face to the left and repeat:**</u> **Asalaamu-alaikum wa rahmat Allah** (Peace be with you and Allah's blessings).

Fajr	2 rakats Sunnah + 2 rakats Fard
Zuhr	4 rakats Sunnah + 4 rakats Fard + 2 rakats Sunnah + 2 rakats Nafilah
Asr	4 rakats Sunnah + 4 rakats Fard
Maghrib	3 rakats Fard + 2 rakats Sunnah + 2 rakats Nafilah
Isha	4 rakats Sunnah + 4 rakats Fard + 2 rakats Sunnah + 2+3+2 rakats Nafilah

Salah consists of obligatory **Fard** rakats and additional but optional **Sunnah** and **Nafilah** rakats that Muhammad ﷺ used to offer. Whatever he said or did is called Sunnah, and the collection of recorded Sunnah is known as **Hadith**.

As well as purifying the soul by bringing us closer to Allah, the physical actions of salah benefit different parts of our body: the eyes, brain, stomach, heart, and other organs. Subhan'Allah!

And remember! To forgive and forget also helps to purify the heart. Without forgiveness faith is incomplete and life for us all would be very gloomy indeed.

The Joy of Giving

Last Friday, the Imam of our mosque delivered an interesting khutbah (sermon) about alms, the giving of money or food to the poor and needy.

"When it comes to spending or giving," he said, "there are squanderers, misers and wise men. The squanders are wasteful and spend freely, but not for charity. The misers do not like spending at all, not even on themselves. They stash their money away where it benefits no one."

"On the other hand, wise men enjoy spending on themselves as well as others. They know that Allah generously rewards those who give charity and that it helps to expiate sins and earn a place in Paradise. They love to share their wealth and they know the joy of giving."

There's a saying that charity begins at home. My dad often visits our neighbour who is old and lives alone; and the other day, he decided to take me along, too.

Mum gave us several magazines she thought might interest him, and some of her homemade cookies. We were going to take a bunch of flowers as well, but then decided an indoor plant would probably last much longer.

Do you remember the lovely pot I kept when we emptied the loft? Well, I had enough money in it from my savings to buy a beautiful coleus plant.

Our neighbour was delighted to see us and liked all the gifts, especially the cookies and the coleus. And when we were leaving, he asked me if I would like to come again for a game of chess, which made me very happy.

You know, children can also give charity. And even a smile is charity because it can make someone feel good. Kind words can, too; and like a smile they don't cost anything.

ZAKAT – the third Pillar of Islam

Zakat means *that which purifies* and is charity money given to the poor and needy. In His infinite bounty, Allah provides for everyone, but according to His wisdom and His will, He gives more to some than others. Those who are better off must give a portion of their wealth, as they can afford, to help those in need. This creates harmony between rich and poor; and when there is harmony in a society there is more tolerance, good will, and less crime.

Zakat-ul-Fitr is compulsory alms given at the end of the holy month of **Ramadhan**.

SAUM – the fourth Pillar of Islam

All adult Muslims who are fit and able must fast in Ramadhan, the ninth month of the Islamic year. Children can fast, too, but it is not compulsory until they reach adolescence. Travellers, the sick or mentally ill, the elderly, little children, and women expecting or nursing babies, are all exempt.

The month of fasting begins with the sighting of the new moon at the beginning of Ramadhan and ends with the sighting of the new moon at the beginning of Shawwal.

It is a month of great blessings. Muslims not only fast but also pray and read the Quran because it was during Ramadhan that Allah sent the Quran down to the lowest heavens, and through the angel Jibril (Gabriel) revealed its first verses to Muhammad.ﷺ

Before they begin each daily fast, Muslims must say in their heart that they intend to keep fast. There is a special prayer they can recite, too: **Wa bisaumi ghadin nawaito min shahri Ramadhan** (I intend to keep the fast tomorrow in the month of Ramadhan).

The fast begins after **suhoor**, a meal taken before sunrise, and ends just before sunset with a meal called **iftar**. It is sunnah to end the fast with dates or water.

There is also a prayer for ending the fast: **Allahumma inni-lakasumtu wa'alla rizqika-aftartu** (Allah, I have kept fast for You, and I am breaking the fast with the food You have blessed me with).

"Sir, is it necessary to say these prayers?" I asked.

"It is better to say them," Sir replied. "But what is most important is our intention. We do not fast to starve ourselves or to show off. We fast only to please Allah. And that is how we can earn the best reward."

"Fasting has many physical and spiritual benefits," Sir continued. "It teaches us discipline and patience. Also, having the willpower to refrain from eating and drinking from sunrise to sunset helps to develop self-control. Fasting also makes us more thankful for the blessing of food and water because we actually experience how it feels to be without them.

"Fasting helps to develop sympathy and empathy for the poor and less fortunate who have very little. Also, the time we normally spend eating or drinking, we can devote to praying or reading the Quran instead."

"The body's digestive system uses a lot of energy, so when we fast our heart, liver, stomach, kidneys and other parts of our body are given a rest."

With the sighting of the new moon, the month of fasting ends. The next day, **Eid-ul-Fitr**, is a day of joyful celebration.

It is the best day of the year. People gather in the mosques for Eid Prayers, and afterwards friends and families get together to chat and enjoy delicious food. Sometimes, there are presents, too.

Journey of a Lifetime

In his lifetime, Prophet Muhammad ﷺ showed his Muslim followers how to perform hajj. The story of hajj, however, begins with **Prophet Ibrahim**, alayhi salaam, who lived on this earth thousands of years ago.

Prophet Ibrahim had a very beautiful wife, Sarah, but after many years they were still childless. Sarah then persuaded him to marry her maidservant, Hajar, who bore him a son they named **Ismail** (Ishmael, alayhi salaam).

Not long after, Sarah became so jealous she told Ibrahim to send them away. Naturally, he was very reluctant, but when Allah ordered him to do what she asked, with the promise that Hajar and Ismail would be provided for, he took them to Mecca; and there he left them, with nothing but some dates and a leather bag of water.

In the scorching heat, the water did not last long, and Ismail began to cry inconsolably. Hajar left him on the ground and ran barefoot between two hills, **al-Safa** and **al-Marwa**, praying to Allah for mercy and looking out for someone to help her. But there was no one.

When she reached the top of al-Marwa for the seventh time, she looked down and was amazed to see an angel standing over Ismail, lightly scraping the sand with the tip of its wings. Suddenly, water sprang from the ground. Hajar raced down the hill and put her hands over the miraculous water. "**Zam! Zam!**" (Stop! Stop!) she said, but the water did not stop.

When travellers learned about the spring, they came to settle there. Hajar was delighted to have company at last and heartily welcomed them. Ibrahim also visited from time to time. When Ismail was about ten years old, he came and asked him to walk with him. Clearly, there was something on his mind; something troubling him. Finally, he spoke.

"My dear son, three times I have seen in a dream that I must sacrifice you. Please tell me what I should do."

"Do as Allah commands you," Ismail calmly replied. "Insha'Allah, you will find me patient."

Ibrahim was now faced with an agonising decision. Should he spare his beloved son and risk displeasing Allah, or should he act upon the dream and sacrifice him? Three times the devil tempted him to ignore the dream, but each time Ibrahim became even more determined to obey his Lord. Finally, he laid Ismail down to sacrifice him.

"O Ibrahim!" Allah called out. "You have fulfilled the dream." And He sent a ram for Ibrahim to slaughter in place of Ismail.

Allah was testing Ibrahim, and he proved that his love for Allah was greater than his love for his son. Perhaps that is why Allah honoured him by calling him *Khalilullah* (God's intimate friend). Allah knows!

Many years later, Allah commanded Ibrahim to build the Sacred House, the Kaaba, which he did with Ismail's help; and as they worked together, building the foundations, they prayed, "Our Lord! Accept from us this duty, make us submissive to You, and show us our ways of worship."

HAJJ – the fifth Pillar of Islam

All Muslims must perform hajj at least once in their lifetime if they are well enough and can afford it. Hajj is the pilgrimage to **al Masjid al-Haram** in Mecca and takes place in the last month of the Islamic year, **Dhul-Hijjah**.

Every year, millions of Muslims from every corner of the world gather in Mecca to perform hajj. Allah forgives all their past sins, listens to their prayers, and rewards them for just being there.

To perform hajj, or lesser hajj called **umrah**, a Muslim must enter a state of purity called **ihram**. Men symbolise ihram by wearing a white, unstitched garment consisting of two cotton sheets or towels, one to cover the upper part of the body, one to cover the lower, usually secured by a belt.

Women wear simple clothes that fully cover the body except for the face, hands, and feet. Ihram's symbolic clothing testifies there is no difference between a rich man or a poor man, a prince or a pauper. It also symbolises purity.

Pilgrims beg forgiveness from Allah as they perform the hajj rituals, following in the footsteps of Ibrahim, his son Ismail, and Prophet Muhammad ﷺ who is a direct descendent of Ismail.

The hajj rituals begin on the 7th day of Dhul-Hijjah and end on the 12th day. After entering a state of ihram, the basic rituals are as follows.

* **Tawaf**: Walking anti-clockwise around the Kaaba seven times.

* **al-Safa and al-Marwah**: Running seven times between the two hills.

* **Mount Arafat**: Pilgrims gather there on the 9th day of Hajj. Known also as the Mountain of Mercy, Mount Arafat is where Prophet Muhammad ﷺ

delivered his farewell sermon. It is also believed to be the place where Adam and Hawwa were reunited and forgiven after being expelled from Paradise.

* **Muzdalifah**: An area between Mina and Arafat. Along the way, pilgrims recite **talbiya**, a special prayer that begins, **Labbaik Allahuma labbaik**! (I am present, O Allah! I am present!). Pilgrims stay there overnight, under the stars.

* **Ramy-al-Jamarat**: Throwing stones at the pillars that represent the devil.

* **Qurbani**: Sacrificing a goat, cow, camel, or sheep, as Prophet Ibrahim did.

* **Shaving or clipping the hair** (men only). Women have a lock of hair cut off.

* **Eid al Adha**: Celebrating the three days of festival.

* **Tawaf-al-Wida**: Circumambulation of the Kaaba to bid farewell.

Pilgrims also visit al Masjid al-Nabawi, The Prophet's Mosque in Medina where Muhammad ﷺ lived in later life, and where he died and was buried.

Friends Forever

I have been promoted to a new class. Humza too! Insha'Allah, friends forever! We also have our good friend Mr Google, which is awesome. He's the best teacher ever!

In our first lesson, he asked, "What do Muslims believe?"

Everyone put their hand up, but Sir chose me. I can't imagine why! Well, if I'm honest, it was probably because I was half standing and madly waving both hands. But I'm glad he did because I knew the answer.

"Muslims believe that Allah is the only Lord of the entire universe. He is the Creator of all things, and none has the right to be worshipped but He."

"Well done, Mustafa! But it is only the first of six main articles of faith."

1. **Belief in the Oneness of Allah**
2. **Belief in Angels**
3. **Belief in the Holy Books**
4. **Belief in the Prophets**
5. **Belief in the Day of Judgement and Life Hereafter**
6. **Belief in Preordainment**

Belief in the Oneness of Allah

A Muslim declares this belief when he recites **La ilaha illallah** (none has the right to be worshipped except Allah). And because Muhammad ﷺ is Allah's prophet, a

Muslim also recites **Muhammadur-rasulullah** (Muhammad ﷺ is the Prophet of Allah).

Allah is Self-Sufficient, which means He has no need of any helper or partner. In salah, we acknowledge this when we recite surah Ikhlas (The Purity):

"He is the One God. God the eternal upon whom all depend. He begets not, nor was He begotten. None can be compared to Him."

To worship Allah, the One and only God, is foremost of all the commandments. The greatest sin is **shirk**, the worship of anyone or anything besides Allah, or to say He has partners. Allah says He will forgive any sin except shirk.

Many commandments are repeated in the Holy Quran. Here is one my mum often reminds me of: **"Your Lord has commanded that ... you show kindness to your parents ... When they reach old age, do not be harsh with them nor turn them away but treat them with kindness and pray: My Lord! Have mercy on them both because they cared for me when I was little."**

I hope I never hurt or disrespect my parents or offend them in any way. Now I understand why Allah tells us to be kind to orphans. Without parents, life cannot be easy, so those who have parents should always cherish and respect them.

Although Allah commands us to love Him, His prophets, and His Creation, He clearly says there is no force in religion. He has given everyone the freedom to choose. We can believe in Allah and follow Him for our own good, or we can disbelieve, follow our own ways, and suffer the consequences.

Prophet Nuh, (Noah, alayhi salaam) lived for 950 years. He was one of Allah's special messengers, but sadly his wife and one of his sons were non-believers.

When Nuh's family and small band of followers, along with their animals, boarded the ark, his wife and son were left behind. When the heavens opened and rain began to flood the earth, Nuh looked back and called out to his son, "Come aboard and Allah will save you!"

"I'm not afraid. I'll climb a mountain," his son shouted back. "I'll be safe there." Moments later, a huge wave engulfed him, and he was drowned.

If you recall the story of Prophet Ibrahim, you will remember that He was so near to Allah, he was called "Khalilullah" (God's intimate friend). How strange that his own father, Azhar, was an idol-worshipper! Even worse, he made idols for a living.

"What are you making?" Ibrahim asked him one day.

"Statues of gods," Azhar proudly replied.

Although he was just a boy, Ibrahim was gifted with wisdom and spiritual awareness. He loathed the grotesque idols that filled the nearby temple and felt ashamed that some were made by his own father. So, he decided to confront him in the hope that he would stop worshipping them and follow the true religion.

"Can these idols see you when you bow to them? Can they hear your prayers or eat the food you offer? Do they benefit you in any way?" he asked.

Azhar exploded with rage. How dare his son question him about the sacred idols! His forefathers had worshipped them. That was enough for him.

"If you criticise my gods again, I will stone you to death," he threatened.

As Ibrahim grew older, he became increasingly concerned about his father's devotion to idols and tried his utmost to persuade him and his people to give them up and follow the One True God, but they stubbornly refused.

One day, he noticed everyone was leaving the temple to attend a pagan festival outside the city. This was the chance he had been waiting for! As an excuse to stay behind, he pretended to be unwell; and when he was sure everyone had gone, he silently slipped into the temple.

"Why don't you eat the offering before you?" he taunted the idols. "What is the matter with you that you do not speak? Why do you not reply?"

He then turned on them and struck them down, smashing them all except the biggest. Placing an axe on the biggest idol's shoulder, he then quietly left.

When the people returned and discovered what had happened there was pandemonium. "Who has done this appalling act?" they wailed.

"Why don't you ask *him*?" Ibrahim mocked, pointing to the biggest idol.

"Don't talk nonsense! You know very well the statues cannot move or talk," they honestly, but foolishly replied.

"Then why do you worship them? Worship Allah Who created us, provides for us, heals us when we are sick, hears and answers our prayers," said Ibrahim.

This was too much! Crazed with rage, they rushed forward chanting, "Burn him! Burn him!"

They built a huge fire and threw Ibrahim into it, but he neither struggled nor cried out. Flames leapt high into the sky and smoke filled the air, blackening the faces of the onlookers and making them hot and sweaty. Calmly, Ibrahim prayed: "**Hasbi Allahu wa-naimul wakeel.**" (Allah is sufficient for us, and He is the Best Disposer of Affairs). And Allah commanded the fire to be cool for him.

Imagine everyone's astonishment when Ibrahim calmly walked out of the fire, his face radiant and completely unharmed!

Amazingly, having witnessed such a miracle, Azhar and his people still refused to give up their idols. But like all prophets, Ibrahim had no power over his people to make them believe. His mission was only to convey Allah's Message, which he had faithfully done. It was now time for him to move on and preach elsewhere.

Belief in Angels

Allah created angels from pure light. They are neither male nor female, and unlike human beings have no freedom of choice. They are Allah's Personal Messengers, bound to obey His every command. They are huge in form with multiple pairs of wings. There are angels before and behind us, watching over us by Allah's command. Countless angels, forever descending and ascending between heaven and earth, each with a special duty to perform.

The Archangel, Jibril, also called *The Angel of Revelations*, is said to be the greatest of them all. Verse by verse, he revealed the Holy Quran to Prophet Muhammad ﷺ. He also came to Maryam (Mary, **radhi'Allahu unha**, May Allah be pleased with her!) to foretell the birth of her son, **Isa** (Jesus, alayhi salaam).

Mikhail, the Angel of Mercy, is responsible for directing rain and winds according to Allah's command. Azra'il, the Angel of Death, oversees the taking of people's souls when they die. The angel Israf'il will blow the Trumpet to announce the end of time on earth. Ridwan guards the Gates of Paradise, and Malik is the main guardian of Hell. The angels Munkar and Nakir will question people about their beliefs when they die. They will ask three questions: Who is your God? Who is your prophet? And what is your religion?

Harut and Marut were angels sent to the people of Babel (Babylon) to teach them a lesson about black magic. Like the sorcerers, they performed magic, but only to demonstrate and warn people that it is a sin.

Recording Angels (Kiraman Katibeen) record every word and deed in a special Book. We each have at least two angels, one on our right, one on our left. On the Day of Judgement, those who believe in the Oneness of God will be given their Book in their right hand. Those who disbelieve will receive it in their left.

How cautious we are when we know someone is watching or listening, or when there are surveillance cameras overhead! However, people and cameras cannot see and hear everything and everywhere, into our homes and other private places. But Allah can.

He is **al-Baseer** (the All-Seeing), **al-Sami** (the All-Hearing), **al-Aleem** (the All-Knowing), and **al-Khabir** (the Aware). There are no hiding places. Wherever we are, Allah sees everything we do and hears everything we say. He even knows what is in our hearts and minds.

Belief in the Holy Books

Throughout the ages, Allah sent prophets to guide us. To some, along with His Divine Message, He also gave a Holy Book. The four Holy Books sent by Allah are the **Taurat**, the **Zabur**, the **Injil**, and the **Quran**.

The Taurat, which consists of the Five Books of the Old Testament, Genesis, Exodus, Leviticus, Numbers and Deuteronomy, was revealed to **Prophet Musa** (Moses, alayhi salaam), but religious scholars rewrote many parts of it to suit their own purpose, thus changing much of the original text.

The Zabur, Book of Psalms, also contained in the Old Testament, is the Holy Book of Songs of Praise revealed to Prophet Dawud (David, alayhi salaam), but this has also undergone change.

The Injil was the Holy Book revealed to Prophet Isa (alayhi salaam). The original Gospel was the divinely inspired message that Isa preached to the Children of Israel. The current Gospel (New Testament) contains only portions of Isa's teachings, much of it having been lost or changed from the original.

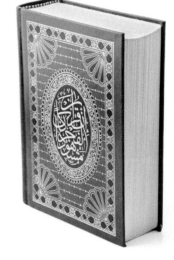

The Quran is the Final Book from Allah and confirmation of all previous revelations. It was revealed to the Last Messenger and Seal of the Prophets, Muhammad ﷺ.

It contains the complete and perfect message from Allah. There are many versions of the Bible, Old and New Testaments, but only one version of the Holy Quran.

More than 1,400 years have elapsed since its revelation and not a word has been changed. Allah has promised to guard it from corruption.

Although Muslims read and follow the Holy Quran, they also believe in the Taurat, Zabur, and Injil because, in their original form, they were the Word of God, sent to guide mankind.

Belief in the Prophets

Man's life on earth began when **Adam** (alayhi salaam) and his wife, Hawwa, were expelled from Paradise for disobeying Allah. Persuaded by Iblis (Satan), they tasted the fruit of the very tree Allah had forbidden them to go near. Since Allah created Adam to rule on earth, falling for temptation while still in Paradise was a warning to be forever wary of Iblis who was also destined for earth. His mission? To lead mankind astray.

Unlike Iblis, who was proud and unrepentant, Adam and Hawwa were deeply ashamed of having disobeyed Allah and begged forgiveness. Allah not only pardoned them, but inspired Adam to become the first prophet on earth.

Allah has since sent prophets to every nation. Endowed with moral excellence, they all taught the same message, to worship the One True God, to obey His Commands and follow His Guidance that we may find peace, happiness, and success in this life and the Hereafter.

Of the thousands of prophets Allah has sent, five were special due to the momentous tasks assigned to them. They are Nuh, Ibrahim, Musa, Isa, and Mohammad ﷺ. Only twenty-five prophets are mentioned in the Holy Quran.

Adam (Adam), **Idris** (Enoch), **Nuh** (Noah), **Hud** (Hud), **Salih** (Salih), **Ibrahim** (Abraham), **Ismail** (Ishmael), **Ishaq** (Isaac), **Lut** (Lot), **Yaqub** (Jacob), **Yusuf** (Joseph), **Shuaib** (Jethro), **Ayyub** (Job), **Musa** (Moses), **Harun** (Aaron), **Dhul-Kifl** (Ezekiel), **Dawud** (David), **Sulaiman** (Solomon), **Ilyas** (Elijah), **Alyasa** (Elisha), **Yunus** (Jonah), **Zakariyya** (Zachariah), **Yahya** (John), **Isa** (Jesus), **Muhammad** ﷺ (sallahu alayhi wasallam).

Unlike other prophets, who were sent to their own nation only, Prophet Muhammad ﷺ was sent to all mankind. He is the Seal of the Prophets, which means no prophet will come after him.

Muhammad's honesty and truthfulness helped him win the hearts of his worst enemies. Being truthful is of utmost importance. Others trust us and become our friends when they know we tell the truth. Lies are the work of the devil and lead to trouble. So, beware!

Belief in the Day of Judgement and Life Hereafter

On the Day of Judgement, life on earth as we know it will come to an end. It will be the beginning of a new life that will never end. On that day, masters will no longer be masters, and slaves will no longer be slaves. No one will own anything, and all will see and acknowledge that there is Only One Master, One Owner of the entire universe, Almighty Allah.

On that day, everyone will be given the Book containing the record of all their deeds, great and small. Allah will judge with absolute justice and will show mercy and forgiveness. According to His pardon and mercy, those who believe in the Oneness of God and whose good deeds weigh heavy in the balance will be blessed with a place in Paradise. **Jinn** will also be judged.

Did you know there are also jinn on this earth? Allah created angels from pure light and jinn from smokeless fire. And then, from mixed clay, He created Adam to be a ruler on the earth. When He had taught Adam the names of everything, He commanded the angels to prostrate to him. All obeyed except Iblis. Although not an angel, but chief of the jinn, Iblis was present when the order to prostrate to Adam was given.

"Why did you not prostrate?" Allah asked him.

"Why should I prostrate to him?" Iblis arrogantly replied. "You made me first from smokeless fire. You made Adam from clay. I am far better than him."

For his pride and defiance, Allah cast Iblis out of Paradise. Since his expulsion, he lurks behind us, forever trying to misguide us with his cunning ways. To follow him is easy, but his is the path that leads to Hell. The path to Paradise is far more difficult. Thankfully, Iblis only has power over those who choose to follow him. He has no power over those who believe in Allah and obey Him. So, we can refuse to listen to him and turn him away.

We cannot normally see jinn, nor can they see us clearly, but they share this earth, living in their own communities in remote areas like forests and mountains. They have the power to travel vast distances at lightning speed and can change their appearance. There are both good and bad jinn. Like us, they have been given freedom of choice, to follow good or evil. That is why they will also be held accountable on the Day of Judgement.

Belief in Preordainment

"Preordainment is probably the most complex of all the main articles of faith to understand," Sir began. "It means that Allah has predetermined what will happen to all His creatures. He knows how long each one of us will live, what we will achieve and whatever good or ill-fortune we will have."

He paused, and there was pin drop silence!

And then, a thunderous *Clang! Clang! Clang!* shattered the quiet, and like frightened sheep we all looked to our shepherd for help. Clearly amused, Sir smiled back at us.

"There's no need to panic," he said, gesturing us to stay calm. "It's only the school bell. It's home time!"

The subject of Preordainment really puzzled me and left me with more questions than answers, so I asked Dad about it. "Why should we make any effort when everything is already decided?"

Dad always has an answer. "Well, I must admit it is baffling," he replied. "But remember, Allah has given us freedom to choose what we say and do. This story might help you to understand."

Long ago, a man was travelling on horseback through a foreign land. Being a pious man, he stopped along the way to pray. A poor beggar was sitting on the ground near the temple door, so the traveller asked him if he would mind his horse while he was inside praying. The beggar agreed.

I'll give him five silver coins for his kindness, the traveller thought as he entered the temple. Prayers over, the traveller looked around for the beggar, but he was nowhere to be seen. And then he discovered his horse's saddle was missing. Leading his horse by the reins, he walked to the nearby town and found a shop where he hoped he could buy a new saddle. And sure enough, the shopkeeper had exactly what he needed.

After examining it, he realised it was in fact his own saddle. When he asked the shopkeeper how he had come by it, he told him a beggar had sold it to him only a short while ago.

"And how much did you pay him?" asked the traveller.

"Five silver coins," the shopkeeper replied.

"So, you see, Mustafa, it was already decided that the beggar would receive five silver coins at the precise moment he did, but he made the wrong choice. Instead of the honest way, he chose to get it the dishonest way.

"Allah has given jinn and mankind the right to choose what they do. Although He has already decreed what will happen, He is **al-Qadir** (the All-Powerful). If we pray and ask Him, He can change things. The story of the people of Nineveh is a wonderful example of this."

The capital city of the Assyrian Empire, Nineveh, was a vibrant, prosperous city with tall buildings and magnificent palaces, but the people were utterly depraved and worshipped idols.

For forty years, **Prophet Yunus** (Jonah, alayhi salaam) preached, urging them to abandon idolatry and mend their wanton ways, but they paid no heed. He gave them one final warning that Allah's punishment would surely come and that all would perish, but recklessly they answered, "Let it come! Let it come!"

Exasperated, Yunus decided to leave them to their fate. As he was approaching the outskirts of the city, the sky suddenly turned red as if on fire. Surely, they are now doomed, he thought, and hurried on towards the shore where he boarded a ship that took him far out to sea.

Fearful of the impending catastrophe, the people of Nineveh clambered to the top of a hill and prayed aloud, sincerely, earnestly begging for forgiveness. Allah pardoned them and the impending disaster was averted.

Meanwhile, Yunus was in great trouble. He had been cast off the ship and swallowed by a huge fish. His punishment, perhaps, for leaving his mission without Allah's command. Allah knows!

Deeply ashamed, Yunus prayed for forgiveness. Commanded by Allah, the fish spewed him out onto the shore. And there he lay, sick and helpless. When at last he opened his eyes, he saw a gourd tree, providing him with shade and sustenance. A blessing from his Lord!

Sometime later, when he was well enough to travel, Yunus went back to Nineveh. He was not only overwhelmed by the genuine welcome he received but amazed to see how the people had changed. They now believed in Allah and openly worshipped Him.

"So, you see," Dad explained. "It is possible for things to change if Allah wills it. And our prayers can change our destiny. Along with good deeds, prayers may increase Allah's blessings and help avoid calamities."

"We might know something about the past, but we know nothing about the future. Allah alone knows what is past, present, and future. He knows everything."

"Imagine yourself standing by a stream watching a log float by. Your eyes follow it as far as you can see, but then it goes out of sight. The log could go peacefully floating on forever or encounter rapids, waterfalls, anything. You do not know because you cannot see ahead or around bends. Similarly, we do not know what will happen tomorrow."

"Dad, you explain things so well but still, it is very puzzling."

"Yes, it is! That is because our knowledge is limited to our earthly existence, whereas Allah's knowledge relates to the entire universe and is infinite."

A Fun Day at School

Does it ever snow where you are? Where I live it does; in winter when it's freezing cold. And the other morning I woke up to discover it had snowed all night.

"Hurray! No school today, Dad! We can play in the snow and make a snowman. Let's see if we can make an even better one than last year."

Dad, however, doesn't like the idea of missing a single day at school, unless there's a very good reason, so he rang the school to find out if it was closed because of the snow. Sadly for me and my plans for playing and making a wonderful snowman, it wasn't.

So, I trudged all the way only to discover very few children had turned up. The rest must have guessed it was a holiday. Lucky them, I thought, feeling rather glum. But then someone threw a snowball at me. And another! I turned to see who it was. My best friend, Humza! And that immediately cheered me up.

Even better, there were no lessons. Sir had arranged some exciting activities instead. He began with a general knowledge quiz. Humza and I were in the same team, and guess what? We won! To end our wonderful day, Sir told some amazing stories. The following is based on a story from the Holy Quran.

The Richest Man in the Land

A very rich man lived with his lovely wife and children in a grand mansion surrounded by beautiful gardens. He also had many orchards, and endless fields of corn with a gentle stream running through.

One day, an old friend came to visit. After showing him around the estate, the rich man invited him onto the veranda for tea. It was late in the afternoon. The sun was going down and the air was filled with the sweet, mingling fragrance of flowers, fruit, and ripening corn.

"Look!" said the rich man, pointing to the fields where the corn, heavy with grain, rippled in the breeze like a golden sea against the bright orange sky.

"Have you ever seen anything more splendid? Soon, we will harvest the corn. It will be a bumper crop for sure."

His friend did not reply. If only he had said *Insha'Allah*, he thought.

That night, without warning, there was a violent storm. Rain and hailstones pounded the earth. Thunder and lightning rocked the skies and the howling wind raged like a wild, ferocious monster across the land, devouring everything in its path. By morning, the storm was over. All was calm. But there was not a flower to be seen. Many fruit trees had been uprooted and the corn was ruined, flattened, and blackened by the wind and hail.

The rich man stood on the veranda, staring in silent disbelief and despair at the awful devastation. In just one night, his fortune had been overturned and he could not understand why. But his wife understood.

"Allah made you the richest man in the land, and He gave us everything. A wonderful home and beautiful, healthy children," she quietly explained, "but when did we ever pray to thank Him? We were too complacent, too busy. Even then, Allah is so kind. The garden and all the crops may be ruined, but we are unharmed, and our house is still standing."

"It's true!" he admitted. "We took Allah's blessings for granted. But it's never too late. Let us beg His forgiveness. And from now on, let us remember to be forever thankful."

The next story is from the Gospel and teaches us that prayer alone is not sufficient. We must also perform good deeds. "Allah is pleased when we help others," Sir explained, "regardless of their colour, race or creed."

The Good Samaritan

A Jew was travelling alone from Jerusalem to Jericho along a desolate and treacherous road where bandits were known to attack, rob and even kill innocent, unsuspecting wayfarers. And as luck would have it, the Jew was attacked. The bandits beat him, took his money and most of his clothes, and left him on the roadside to die.

Soon after, a priest came along the same road. He saw the bleeding, half-naked man, but crossed to the other side and hurried on his way. The bandits could be close by, he thought, and might attack him too, so it would be foolish to stop for even a moment.

Later, a temple servant came that way. Like the priest, he had come from the synagogue, from the worship of the God of love and kindness, but he also hurried past the wounded man even though he knew he was a fellow Jew.

Not long after, a Samaritan riding a donkey passed by. Samaritans were immigrants, despised by the Jews because they were of a different race and religion, but seeing the wounded man he immediately stopped to help him.

There but for the grace of God go I, he said to himself, meaning that could have been me. He gave the man some water, helped him onto his donkey, and took him to the nearest inn where he spent the night looking after him.

The next day, the Samaritan prepared to continue his journey. After settling his account with the innkeeper, he paid him extra to take care of the wounded man. "If this is not enough, I'll pay the rest next time I'm here," he promised.

The innkeeper was curious to know why he was going out of his way to help a stranger. "Always do as you would be done by," the Samaritan replied. "In other words, treat your fellow men as you would like them to treat you. And for the love of God, always have empathy and compassion for others."

The next story is also from the Gospel.

The Widow and the Two Mites

One day, Prophet Isa (alayhi salaam) was sitting with his disciples near the door of the synagogue. He watched as an old woman quietly slipped two mites, coins of the lowest value, into the wooden collection bowl as she left the synagogue. Several very wealthy men in their ostentatious robes followed and each dropped a handful of coins into the bowl, making sure they made a loud clanging sound as they fell.

When all the worshippers had left, Isa turned to his disciples. "Do you know, the old woman has put more money into the charity bowl than anyone else."

His disciples were puzzled. They, too, had seen her put only two mites into the bowl. Isa then explained. "The rich men gave just a little of their vast wealth and they gave it to show off, whereas the old woman, a poor widow, gave nearly all she had, and she gave it for love of God."

Allah is **al-Baseer** (the All-Seeing) and **al-Aleem** (the All-Knowing). He sees what we give and knows what we have and can afford. And He is **ash-Shakur** (the Appreciative). He is pleased when we give without show and generously rewards us when we put aside our own desires to perform our duties or care for others. The next story is about a man who did just that.

The Shepherd and the Angel

There was once an old man who lived alone in a little cottage on a hillside. The people of the nearby village loved and respected him and called him "the shepherd" because, for as long as anyone could remember, he had always kept goats and sheep. He was kind and gentle and knew how to cure most common ailments with his herbal medicine. He was generous, too, and refused to take money from the villagers who were mostly poor folk.

"The herbs I use to make medicine are not mine," he would tell them. "They are a gift from God, so how can I take money for something that doesn't belong to me? Besides, I have everything I need and all that I desire."

From dawn to dusk, the shepherd's humble abode was a haven for the poor. Occasionally, well-to-do people came to him for medicine, and he gratefully took the money they offered, to use for those in need.

Now, when the shepherd said he had all that he desired, it was not entirely true. He had a secret longing to be blessed, just once in his lifetime, with a divine vision. Resigned to the probability that it might never happen, he went about his work, tending the sheep and goats, gathering herbs for medicine, and helping the poor. And he prayed.

Early one morning, while he was praying, his tiny room was suddenly filled with light so pure and bright, it took his breath away. Tears of joy filled his weary eyes as slowly, through the brightness, he could see the still, silent form of an angel. At last, his secret longing had been fulfilled.

He was about to look up to see the angel's face when there was a sudden, urgent knocking at the door. For a moment, he was tempted to ignore it or shout, "Go away!" But he knew it must be the little orphan boy who came early every morning for milk and food. Perhaps he will come back later, he thought. But the boy lived far away and would not come again. So, in his heart he knew he must leave the blessed vision and answer the urgent knocking at the door. Despite his heavy heart, he smiled kindly at the little orphan boy as he handed him his daily share of milk and bread.

The angel must have gone, he thought, as he slowly walked back to his room. But oh, what joy! When he opened the door, the angel was still standing there, awaiting his return. He looked up, and through the dazzling light, he saw the angel's face. The angel smiled and was gone, but the warmth, the beauty of that smile touched the old man's heart and stayed with him forever.

Next, is the story of a very rich man who denied Allah's blessings.

A Most Ungrateful Man

Prophet Musa (alayhi salaam) had a very clever relative named Qarun whose God-given talents had enabled him to earn much wealth. He had countless chests full of treasures and a chain of keys to unlock them that was so heavy he could not lift it. With his head held high, and his long robes trailing behind him, he was often seen dragging the hefty chain of keys along the ground.

Qarun became one of the chief advisors of King Firaun who cleverly used him to spy on his own people, the Bani Israel (Children of Israel). Firaun hated the Bani Israel and persecuted them no end because they worshipped only Allah, the One True God and refused to bow down to him.

Many people envied Qarun for his wealth and power and wished to be like him. He was not a good man, however. He knew the Taurat by heart but did not practise its teachings. And he was jealous of Musa and his brother, Harun. Why had they been chosen to lead Bani Israel? They were not rich, but he was. God should have chosen him instead.

Musa explained that it was God's will, so he should accept it. He also told him that his success was due to God's blessings and advised him to give Zakat and share his wealth with those less fortunate so that he may earn reward from God.

Qarun stubbornly refused. His wealth had nothing to do with God, he argued. It was all due to his own ingenuity and hard work. He was so proud, greedy, and miserly; nothing could ever persuade him to part with his treasures. But his pride, ingratitude and miserliness were his undoing. One day, Allah caused the ground beneath him to open and swallow him up, along with his home and all his treasures.

If I had told a story, it would have been the story of Dawud and Jalut (David and Goliath). When the two armies of Talut (King Saul) and Jalut met on the battlefield, Dawud amazed everyone by challenging Jalut to single combat.

Dawud was just a lad with stones and a sling for a weapon, and Jalut was a fearsome, giant of a man in full body armour. But the brave, confident Dawud had one thing Jalut lacked. Complete faith in Allah!

"Have you come out to play or are you tired of life already?" Jalut bellowed. "Come then! And I'll kill you with a single swipe of my sword."

"Today, you will see it is not the sword that kills but the Will and Power of Allah," Dawud boldly shouted back. Mighty words indeed!

And then, with one shot from his sling, with just one small stone, Dawud hit the not-so-mighty Jalut on the head and knocked him down. Dawud rushed forward and the soldiers followed, ready and eager to crush the enemy.

Dawud took the sword from Jalut's hand and killed him with it. Seeing their mighty warrior lying dead on the ground, Jalut's army panicked. Those who managed to escape the soldiers' swords fled to the hills.

That's the story I would have told.

Anyway, I'm really glad it snowed. We had an awesome day. Those who stayed at home were not so lucky after all, were they. In fact, when they find out what they missed, I think they'll be sorry they didn't come to school.

The Year of the Elephant

Prophet Muhammad ﷺ, the last and final prophet, was born in Mecca in the land of Arabia. Since the Arabs had no calendar at that time, the exact date of his birth is not known, but records show he was born on a Monday at around midday in the beginning of Rabi-ul-awwal. The year was 570 C.E., also known as the Year of the Elephant because of a particular event involving elephants that took place. Here is the story.

Abrahah, the Christian ruler of Yemen, was envious of Mecca's popularity as a trade centre and place of worship. He wanted to divert Mecca's trade to San'a, the capital city of Yemen, so he built a magnificent cathedral and ordered all the Yemeni Arabs to make pilgrimage there instead.

The order was ignored. Worse still, in defiance, a man from the Quraysh tribe of Mecca defecated inside the cathedral, soiling the floor and walls. Enraged by this despicable act, Abrahah vowed to take revenge. His plan! To demolish the Kaaba and wipe out Mecca's fame forever.

He set off with his mighty army, which included about twenty elephants, and marched towards Mecca. The people of Mecca had never seen an elephant before, so when Abrahah arrived with his massive army and mighty beasts they were dumbstruck.

Abrahah planned to use Mahmud, the biggest and strongest elephant, to pull down the walls of the Kaaba. However, the moment they reached the outskirts of Mecca something astonishing happened.

Mahmud stopped abruptly, got down on his knees and refused to move. After a lot of coaxing, they managed to get him on his feet, but although he walked willingly in the direction of Yemen or Syria, whenever they led him towards Mecca he knelt again.

They poked and prodded him with long spears, but Mahmud still refused to take one step towards Mecca and the Sacred House.

And then another amazing thing happened. Flocks of strange birds suddenly covered the sky, and as they flew over Abrahah's army they pelted the soldiers with tiny clay pebbles that struck like hand grenades and killed them. The elephants panicked and fled. Abrahah also fled but died just before reaching home.

Muhammad's parents were Abdullah and Aminah. Abdullah was one of the youngest of the many sons of Abdul-Muttalib, custodian of the sacred Kaaba. Aminah was the noble daughter of Wahb, chief of the Bani Zahrah tribe.

Not long after the marriage, Abdullah set off on a trade journey to Syria. On the return journey, feeling a little unwell, he decided to stay at a relative's house in Medina, known then as **Yathrib**. However, his health took an unexpected turn for the worse and he passed away. Everyone was shocked and filled with grief and disbelief. Abdullah was only twenty-five years old and had left home hale and hearty. Now he was gone.

Aminah grieved not only for her husband but for the unborn child he would never see. According to a dream she had some weeks before the birth, she named her baby Muhammad ﷺ, which means *The Praised One*.

To begin with, Aminah looked after her baby. Later, however, as was the custom among the elite Quraysh, she entrusted him to Halima who belonged to a noble Bedouin tribe. Life on the desert plains with its wide-open spaces and fresh air was preferable to the over-crowded city where diseases quickly spread. The Bedouins were also renowned and admired for their pure Arabic speech. Halima was extremely fond of Muhammad,ﷺ so was absolutely delighted when she was allowed to keep him longer than was first agreed.

When Muhammad ﷺ was about six years old, Aminah decided to take him to Medina to meet her relatives. Sadly, however, on the homeward journey at a place called Abwa about 65 kilometres from Mecca, Aminah fell gravely ill. Three days later, she died.

Muhammad's grandfather, Abdul-Muttalib became the little boy's guardian. He loved him dearly and took very special care of him, but not for long. He was very old and frail and died just two years later. Muhammad's paternal uncle, Abu Talib, then became his guardian, protector, and loyal friend.

When he was twenty-five years old, Muhammad ﷺ married Khadijah, a relative and wealthy businesswoman. She was also known as *Tahira* (The Pure). Their marriage was a blissful one and they were blessed with two sons, who sadly died in infancy, and four daughters.

Muhammad ﷺ would often meditate and pray in the mountain cave of Hira on the outskirts of Mecca. It was during the month of Ramadhan, when he was about forty years old, that the angel Jibril appeared to him in the cave and revealed the first words of the Quran; words in Arabic because Arabic was the native language of Muhammad ﷺ and his people. Later, Allah commanded him to spread the message of Islam.

His loving wife, Khadijah, was the first to embrace Islam. Thereafter, she spent all her wealth supporting her husband's mission and is rightly called Mother of the Believers (radhi'Allahu unha, May Allah be pleased with her!).

From then onwards, Muhammad's life was in danger. Whilst many clansmen supported him out of tribal loyalty, most refused to give up their idols and became his enemies. Still, Muhammad ﷺ was always full of love and compassion, even for those who wished him harm.

His paternal uncle, Abu Lahab, abused him at every opportunity, and his wife, Umm Jamil, composed hateful poems. She would also tie bundles of thorny sticks together with woven strands of palm leaves and spread them along the paths where Muhammad ﷺ walked. But he never uttered a word of complaint.

Muhammad ﷺ was always kind to animals. Having been a shepherd, he knew how to take care of camels, goats, and sheep. And he would often deliver a sermon with his favourite cat, Muezza, nestled in his lap. Once, he found her asleep on the sleeve of his robe. He did not have the heart to disturb her, so he quietly cut off the sleeve and went for prayer wearing a robe with one sleeve missing.

Even when he was the most powerful man in Arabia, Prophet Muhammad ﷺ led a very simple life. He would milk the goats, mend his own clothes, repair his own shoes, and share his meals with his servants. He liked to eat barley bread, dates, watermelon, yogurt, cucumber, honey, milk, and occasionally meat. If he wasn't hungry, he didn't eat.

When travelling, he would often allow a servant or companion to sit on his camel while he walked alongside.

After **Hijra**, the migration from Mecca to Medina, the Prophet settled there. He is buried in **al Masjid al-Nabawi**, the Mosque of the Prophet, Medina.

A Gift for All

Allah sent a very special gift to enlighten all mankind. The Holy Quran!

A Book of divine truth, wisdom, and guidance, it is the Word of our Creator, Almighty Allah, and His Final Message to us.

Throughout His Holy Book, it is Allah Himself who speaks directly to us.

He also sent a succession of prophets to guide mankind and each one preached in the language of his people. To some prophets, Allah also revealed Holy Books containing His laws and commandments, stories, and parables.

The Quran was revealed in Arabic to Prophet Muhammad ﷺ, His Last and Final Messenger. Since it is not my mother tongue, I am learning Arabic to help me understand the Holy Quran. I am also reading an English translation.

I want to know what Allah tells us about Himself, our life on earth, what to do, what not to do, and how to earn His blessings. All these answers are in the Holy Quran and Hadith, the recorded words and actions of Prophet Muhammad ﷺ.

Remember! The Holy Quran was not sent to any one nation but to all the people of the world. Black and white, of east and west, north, and south! And it is for you and me, so read it every day.

Alhamdulillah! We have now come to the end of our amazing journey. I hope you have enjoyed it. I certainly have. Keep searching for knowledge. You will be amazed by what you discover and what you learn. From the cradle onwards, learning never ends. That's what my mum always says. And it's true! I learn something new every day.

Time now to say, *Goodbye!* (God be with you!)

Or **Allah Hafiz**! (May Allah be your Guardian!)

Or, as my family always says, **Fi Aman'Allah**! (May you be in Allah's protection!)

I hope you will remember me, your Muslim friend,

Mustafa

Words of Wisdom

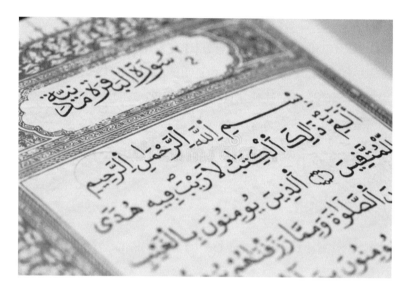

The Quran has 114 surahs or chapters.

The first surah, **al Fatihah** (The Opening), is a prayer, praising Allah and asking for guidance.

Bismillah ir-Rahman ir-Rahim! Alhamdulillahi Rabbil Alamin, ir-Rahman ir-Rahim, Malaiki Yaumideen. Iyyaka n'abudu wa iyyka nastaeen. Ihdi nasiratal mustaqeem, siratal ladhina an 'amta alaiheem ghairil maghdubi alaihim walad dua'leen (ameen).

In the name of God, the Lord of Mercy, the Giver of Mercy! Praise belongs to God, Lord of All the Worlds, the Lord of Mercy, the Giver of Mercy, and Master of the Day of Judgement. You alone we worship and You alone we ask for help. Guide us to the straight path; the path of those whom You have favoured and who did not earn Your anger nor went astray (O' Allah, accept our prayer).

Quotations from the Quran

There is Only One God, Allah

"Your God is the One God; there is no God except Him, the Infinitely Merciful, the Lord of Mercy." al-Baqarah (The Cow), 2: 163.

"If there had been in the heavens or earth any gods but Him, both heavens and earth would be in ruins. God, Lord of the Throne, is far above the things they say (about Him)." al-Anbiya (The Prophets), 21: 22.

"God has never had a child. Nor is there any God beside Him. If there were, each god would have taken his creation aside and tried to overcome others. May God be exalted above what they describe!" al-Mu'minun (The Believers), 23: 91.

The Quran is a Book of Guidance

"This is the Book about which there is no doubt; guidance for those who are mindful of God, believe in the unseen, keep up the prayer, and give out of what We have provided for them; those who believe in the revelation sent down to you (Muhammad) and in what was sent before you (to Musa, Dawud and Isa), and who believe in the Hereafter." al-Baqarah, 2: 2–5.

"This is a blessed Book which We have sent down, so follow it and be mindful of your Lord that you may receive mercy." al-An'am (Livestock), 6: 155.

"We have sent down the Quran and will protect it." al-Hijr (The Rocky Tract), 15: 9.

"In matters of faith, He has laid down for you the same commandment that He gave to Nuh (Noah), which We have revealed to you (O Muhammad) and which We enjoined on Ibrahim (Abraham), Musa (Moses) and Isa (Jesus)." al-Shura (Consultation), 42: 13.

True Believers

"The believers, both men and women, support each other; they order what is right and forbid what is wrong; they keep up the prayer and pay the prescribed alms; they obey God and His Messenger..." al-Tawba (Repentance), 9: 71 and 72.

"Those who believe and perform good deeds are the best of people. Their reward from their Lord is everlasting gardens with flowing streams where they will stay forever." al-Bayyina (Clear Evidence), 98: 7.

"Who could be better in religion than those who direct themselves wholly to God, who do good deeds and follow the religion of Ibrahim who was true in faith and whom God took as an intimate friend." al-Nisa (Women), 4: 125.

Friends of the Believers

"God knows your enemies best. God is sufficient to protect and help you." al-Nisa, 4: 45.

"Your true friends are God, His Messenger, and the believers; those who keep up the prayer, pay the prescribed alms, and bow down (to God). Those who turn for protection to God, His Messenger, and the believers (are God's party). God's party is sure to triumph." al-Ma'ida (The Feast), 5: 55 and 56.

Allah is All-Powerful

"God has created the heavens and the earth for a true purpose. There surely is a sign in this for those who believe." al-Ankabut (The Spider), 29: 44.

"When He intends a thing, He says, 'Be!' And it is." Ya Sin, 36: 82.

"God has control of the heavens and the earth; He creates whatever He will ... He is All Knowing and All Powerful." al-Shura, 42: 49 and 50.

"The creation of the heavens and the earth is indeed greater than the creation of mankind; yet most of mankind know not." al-Ghafir (The Forgiver), 40: 57.

Allah is Near

"We created man. We know what his soul whispers to him: We are closer to him than his jugular vein." Qaaf, 50: 16.

"(O Prophet) if My servants ask you about Me, I am near. I respond to those who call Me, so let them respond to Me and believe in Me so that they may be guided." al-Baqarah, 2: 186.

Allah's Knowledge

"Say, (O Prophet) if the entire ocean were ink for writing the words of my Lord, it would run dry before those words were exhausted; even if We were to add another ocean to it." al-Kahf (The Cave), 18: 109.

"If all the trees on earth were pens and all the seas with seven more seas besides (were ink), still God's words would not be exhausted." Luqman (A wise man named Luqman), 31: 27.

The Importance of Prayer

"I created jinn and mankind only to worship Me." al-Dhariyat (Scattering Winds), 51: 56.

"Remember Job (Ayyub), when he cried to his Lord, 'Suffering has truly afflicted me, but You are the Most Merciful of the merciful.' We answered him, removed his suffering, and restored his family to him along with more like them, as an act of grace from Us and a reminder for all who serve Us." al-Anbiya, 21: 83.

"Your Lord says, Call on Me and I will answer you." al-Mu'min (The Believer), 40: 60.

"Keep up regular prayer, for prayer is obligatory for the believers at prescribed times." al-Nisa, 4: 103.

Beware of the Devil

"O Believers! Do not follow in Satan's footsteps; if you do so, he will incite you to indecency and wickedness." al-Nur (Light), 24: 21.

"He (Satan) has no power over those who believe and trust in their Lord; his power is only over those who befriend him and who, because of him, ascribe partners with God." al-Nahl (The Bee), 16: 98 – 100.

"Whoever chooses Satan as a friend instead of God is utterly ruined: he makes them promises and raises false hopes, but his promises are nothing but deception. Such people will have Hell for their home and will find no escape from it." al-Nisa, 4: 118 – 121.

"With intoxicants and gambling, Satan seeks only to create enmity and hatred among you, and to stop you from remembering God and prayer." al-Mai'da, 5: 91.

Beware of Worldly Distractions

"The love of desirable things is made alluring for men; women, children, amassing of gold and silver treasures, fine horses, livestock and farmland; these may be the comforts of this life, but God has the best place to return to." al-Imran (The family of Imran), 3: 14.

"Believers! Do not let your wealth and your children distract you from remembering God; those who do so will be the ones who lose." al-Munafiqun (The Hypocrites), 63: 9.

"Neither your wealth nor your children will bring you nearer to Us, but those who believe and perform good deeds will have multiple rewards for what they have done and will live safely in the lofty dwellings of Paradise." Saba (Sheba), 34: 37.

Manners and Behaviour

"Worship God; join nothing with Him. Be good to your parents, relatives, orphans, the needy, neighbours near and far, travellers in need, and to your slaves or servants. God does not like arrogant, boastful people who are miserly and order other people to be the same, hiding the bounty God has given them." al-Nisa, 4: 36 and 37.

"Your Lord has commanded that you should worship none but Him, and that you be kind to your parents. If either or both reach old age with you, say no word that shows impatience with them and do not be harsh with them, but speak to them respectfully and care for them with kindness and humility; and say: Lord, have mercy on them, just as they cared for me when I was little." al-Isra (The Night Journey), 17: 23 and 24.

"… if a person is patient and forgives, this is one of the greatest things." al-Shura (The Consultation), 42: 43.

"Believers, no one group of men should jeer at another, who may after all be better than them; no one group of women should jeer at another, who may after all be better than them; do not speak ill of one another; do not use offensive nicknames for one another...

"Avoid making too many assumptions. Some assumptions are sinful. And do not spy on one another or speak ill of people behind their backs: would any of you like to eat the flesh of your dead brother? No, you would hate it. So be mindful of God." al-Hujurat (The Private Rooms) 49: 11 and 12.

"You who believe, intoxicants, gambling, idolatrous practices, and (divining with) arrows for seeking luck or making decisions are an abomination of Satan's handiwork, so shun them that you may prosper." al-Ma'ida, 5: 90.

"Anyone who commits an offence or a sin and then blames it on some innocent person has burdened himself with a falsehood and a great sin." al-Nisa, 4: 112.

"Do not mix truth with falsehood or hide the truth when you know it." al-Baqarah, 2: 42.

"My people, in fairness, give full measure and weight. Do not withhold from people things that are rightly theirs and do not spread corruption in the land." Hud, 11: 85.

"O' believers! Do not enter other people's houses until you have asked permission to do so and greeted those inside; that is best for you … and if you find no one in, do not enter unless you have been given permission to do so. And if you are told to go away, do so; that is more proper for you." al-Nur, 24: 27 and 28.

"Do not strut arrogantly about the earth: you cannot break it open, nor match the mountains in height." al-Isra, 17: 37.

"Do not say of anything, I shall do that tomorrow, without adding, 'God willing,' and whenever you forget, remember your Lord and say: May my Lord guide me closer to what is right." al-Kahf, 18: 23 and 24.

"Children of Adam! We have given you garments to hide your nakedness and as adornment for you. Being aware of God is the best garment of all." al-A'raf (The Heights), 7: 26 and 27.

Food and Drink

"You are forbidden to eat carrion (that which dies naturally), blood, the flesh of swine (pigs, hogs and boars), any animal over which any name other than God's has been invoked; any animal strangled, or victim of a violent blow or fall, or savaged by a beast of prey, unless you can slaughter it (in the correct way) while it is still alive; also forbidden is an animal slaughtered for idols." al-Ma'ida, 5: 3.

"People, eat what is good and lawful from the earth ... You who believe, eat the good things We have provided for you and be grateful to God." al-Baqarah, 2: 168 and 173.

"Then eat all kinds of fruit and follow the ways made easy for you by your Lord. Behold, from their bellies (the bees) comes a liquid of varying shades in which there is healing for mankind." al-Nahl, 16: 69.

"They ask you (Prophet) about intoxicants and gambling. Say: There is a great sin in both, and some benefit for people, but the sin is greater than the benefit." al-Baqarah, 2: 219.

Charity

"Those who spend their wealth in God's cause are like grains of corn that produce seven ears (seed-bearing spikes), each bearing a hundred grains. God gives multiple increase (of reward) to whoever He wishes." al-Baqarah, 2: 261.

"Give relatives their due, and the needy, and travellers, and do not squander your wealth wastefully. The squanderers are like Satan's brothers; and Satan is most ungrateful to his Lord ... but if you turn them down (those who need help from you), then at least speak some words of comfort to them." al-Isra, 17: 26 – 28.

"None of you (believers) will attain true piety unless you give of what you cherish: whatever you give, God knows about it very well." al-Imran, 3: 92.

"You who believe, do not cancel out your charitable deeds with reminders and hurtful words." al-Baqarah, 2: 264.

"If you give charity openly, it is good, but if you keep it secret and give to the needy in private that is better and will atone for some of your bad deeds." al-Baqarah, 2: 271.

Accountability

"Whether you reveal or conceal your thoughts, God will call you to account for them. He will forgive whoever He will and punish whoever He will. He has power over all things." al-Baqarah, 2: 284.

"We have bound each human's destiny to his neck. On the Day of Resurrection, We shall bring out a record for each of them, which they will find wide open. Read your record. Today, your own soul is enough to calculate your account. ... No soul will bear another's burden." al-Isra, 17: 13 –15.

"We will set up scales of justice for the Day of Resurrection so that no one can be wronged in the least, and if there should be even the weight of a mustard seed, We shall bring it out. We take excellent account." al-Anbiya, 21: 47.

"Whoever has done a good deed will have it ten times to his credit, but whoever has done a bad deed will be repaid only with its equivalent." al-An'am, 6: 160.

Prophet Isa (Jesus, alayhis-salaam)

"He (Jesus) said, 'I am a servant of God. He has granted me the Scripture, made me a prophet; made me blessed wherever I may be. He commanded me to pray, give alms as long as I live, and cherish my mother.' ... such was Jesus, son of Mary. (This is) a statement of truth about which they doubt: it would not befit God to have a child. He is far above that. When He decrees something, He says only, 'Be!' And it is!" Maryam (Mary), 19: 30 – 35.

"Jesus, son of Mary, said, 'Children of Israel, I am sent to you by God, confirming the Torah that came before me and giving good news of a messenger to follow me whose name will be Ahmad (one of Prophet Muhammad's names)." al-Saff (The Ranks), 61: 6.

"And because they disbelieved and uttered a terrible slander against Mary and said, 'We have killed the Messiah, Jesus, son of Mary, the Messenger of God.' (They did not kill him, nor did they crucify him, though it was made to appear like that to them ... they certainly did not kill him. No! God raised him up to Himself)." al-Nisa, 4: 157 and 158.

Prophet Muhammad ﷺ (sallallahu alayhi wasallam)

"The Messenger of God (Muhammad) is an excellent model (to follow) for those of you who put your hope in God and the Last Day and remember Him often." al-Ahzab (The Joint Forces), 33: 21.

"Muhammad is not the father of any one of you men; he is God's Messenger and the Seal of the Prophets." al-Azhab, 33: 40.

"Whoever obeys the Messenger, obeys God." al-Nisa, 4: 80.

"It was He who sent His Messenger with guidance and the religion of Truth, to show that it is above all (other) religions. God suffices as a witness: Muhammad is the Messenger of God." al-Fath (Triumph), 48: 28 and 29.

Life and Death

"We decreed to the Children of Israel that if anyone kills a person, unless in retribution for murder or for spreading corruption in the land, it is as if he kills all mankind, while if anyone saves a life it is as if he saves the life of all mankind." al-Ma'ida, 5: 32.

"Every soul is certain to taste death: We test you all through the bad and the good; and to Us you will all return." al-Anbiya, 21: 35.

"Did you think you would enter the Garden (Paradise) without God first proving which of you would struggle for His cause and remain steadfast? al-Imran, 3: 142.

"You are sure to be tested through your possessions and persons." al-Imran, 3: 186.

"No soul may die except with God's permission at a predestined time." al-Imran, 3: 145.

Life in Paradise

"Here is a picture of the Garden promised to the pious: rivers of water forever pure, rivers of milk forever fresh, rivers of wine, a delight for those who drink it; rivers of honey, clear and pure, (all) flow in it; there they will find fruit of every kind; and they will find forgiveness from their Lord." Muhammad, 47: 15.

"(Those foremost in good deeds) will enter lasting Gardens where they will be adorned with bracelets of gold and pearls, where they will wear silk garments. They will say: Praise be to God, Who has separated us from all sorrow! Our Lord is truly Most Forgiving, Most Appreciative. He has, in His bounty, settled us in the Everlasting Home where no toil or fatigue will touch us." Fatir (The Creator), 35: 33 – 35.

"They will sit on couches, feeling neither scorching heat nor biting cold, with shady branches spread above them and clusters of fruit hanging close at hand. They will be served with silver plates and gleaming silver goblets according to their desire; and they will be given a drink infused with ginger from a spring called Salsabil." al-Insan (Man), 76: 12 – 18.

"God has promised the believers, both men and women, Gardens graced with flowing streams where they will remain; good, peaceful homes in Gardens of lasting bliss; and greatest of all, God's good pleasure. That is the supreme triumph." al-Tawba, 9: 72.

The Perfect Religion

"This day, I have perfected your religion for you, completed My blessing upon you, and chosen as your religion Islam (total devotion to God)." al-Ma'ida, 5: 3.

"If anyone seeks a religion other than complete devotion to God (Islam), it will not be accepted from him; he will be one of the losers in the Hereafter." al-Imran, 3: 85.

Glossary

Adhan: Muslim call for prayer

Alhamdulillah: All praise belongs to God

Allah Hafiz: May Allah be your guardian!

Allahu-Akbar: Allah is the greatest

Alayhi salaam: Peace be upon him!

Al-Marwa: a hill in Mecca

Al-Safa: another hill in Mecca

As-salaamu-alaikum: Peace be with you!

Asr: obligatory afternoon prayer

Bismillah ir-Rahman ir-Rahim: (I begin) with the name of God the Lord of Mercy, the Giver of Mercy.

Eid-ul-Adhar: three-day festival celebrated after Hajj

Eid-ul-Fitr: day of celebration at end of Ramadhan, the month of fasting

Fajr: compulsory prayer before sunset

Fard: compulsory prayer

Fi-Aman'Allah: May you be in Allah's protection!

Hadith: recorded sayings of Prophet Muhammad ﷺ

Hajj: pilgrimage to Mecca during month of Dhul Hijjah

Hijra: migration of Muslims from Mecca to Medina

Iftar: meal taken to break the daily fast during Ramadhan

Imam: leader of a mosque, usually a learned Islamic scholar

Injil: Gospels of the New Testament revealed to Isa (Jesus)

Insha'Allah: if Allah wills it

Iqamah: announcement that prayers are about to begin

Isha: compulsory evening prayer

Islam: peace and submission to God; the final and perfect religion

Jazakallahu khairan: may Allah reward you with goodness

Jibril: Gabriel, the Angel of Revelations

Jinn: earthly beings made from smokeless fire

Jummah: Friday, Muslims' day of congregational worship

Kaaba: House of Allah in Mecca

Kalimah: the fundamentals of a Muslim's beliefs

Kalimah Tayyab: Word of Purity

Khalilullah: God's intimate friend (title given to Ibrahim)

Khutbah: sermon delivered by Imam of the mosque every Friday

Maghrib: compulsory prayer after sunset

Masha'Allah: whatever Allah wills (decrees)

Masjid al-Haram: sacred mosque in Mecca, home of the Kaaba

Masjid al-Nabawi: Holy Prophet's mosque in Medina

Muezzin: person who announces the call to prayer

Muslim: follower of the religion of Islam

Muzdalifah: an area between Mina and Arafat

Nafilah: optional prayer

Qiblah: direction towards Kaaba, to which all Muslims face when they pray

Quran: Muslims' Holy Book revealed to Prophet Muhammad ﷺ

Qurbani: sacrificing a sheep, goat, cow, or camel

Rakat: from standing to the two prostrations in prayer

Ramadhan: 9th month of Islamic year and month of fasting

Ramy-al-Jamarat: stoning the devil

Rasul: a prophet to whom a Holy Book was revealed

Salah: obligatory five daily prayers

Saum: fasting during the month of Ramadhan

Shahadah: declaration of faith in Islam

Shirk: the worship of any being or thing, in place of or besides Allah

Subhan'Allah: glorified is Allah

Suhoor: meal before sunrise, before daily fast begins in Ramadhan

Sunnah: what the Holy Prophet said and did or approved of

Taharah: spiritual purity

Talbiya: a special prayer pilgrims recite

Taurat: books of Old Testament revealed to Musa (Moses)

Tawaf: circumambulation of the Kaaba

Tawaf-al-Wida: farewell circumambulation of the Kaaba

Umrah: lesser pilgrimage to Mecca

Wa-alaikum as-salaam: and Peace be with you, too

Wa-rahmatullahi wa-barakatuh: and mercy of Allah and His blessings

Wudu: special ablution Muslims perform before prayer

Yarhamuk Allah: may Allah have mercy on you

Yathrib: old name for Medina

Zabur: Book of Psalms revealed to Prophet Dawud (David)

Zakat: the giving of charity money (alms) for the poor and needy

Zakat-ul-Fitr: alms given at the end of Ramadhan

Zam Zam: miracle spring in Mecca

Zohr: compulsory midday prayer

Printed in the United States
by Baker & Taylor Publisher Services